CITIES OF THE
WORLD

LOS ANGELES

BY R. CONRAD STEIN

CHILDREN'S PRESS®
A Division of Grolier Publishing
New York London Hong Kong Sydney
Danbury, Connecticut

CONSULTANTS

Philip J. Ethington
Associate Professor of History
University of Southern California
Los Angeles

Linda Cornwell
Coordinator of School Quality and Professional Improvement
Indiana State Teachers Association

Project Editor: Downing Publishing Services
Design Director: Karen Kohn & Associates, Ltd.
Photo Researcher: Jan Izzo

Library of Congress Cataloging-in-Publication Data
Stein, R. Conrad
     Los Angeles / by R. Conrad Stein.
      p. cm. — (Cities of the world)
Includes bibliographical references and index.
Summary: Describes the history, culture, daily life, food, people, sports,
and points of interest in the seat of Los Angeles County, California,
the second largest city in the United States.
     ISBN 0-516-22242-2 (lib. bdg.)   0-516-27283-7 (pbk.)
     1. Los Angeles (Calif.)—Juvenile literature. [1. Los Angeles (Calif.)]
I. Title. II. Series: Cities of the world (New York, N.Y.)
    F869.L84 S74 2001
    979.4'94—dc21
                         00-043120

GROLIER
PUBLISHING

TABLE OF CONTENTS

Ride the elevator to the observation tower at the top of the Los Angeles City Hall. On a clear day (and those can be rare), you will see a distance of almost 30 miles (48 kilometers). Yet you will not see the end of Los Angeles. The city is an ocean of buildings and highways. Greater Los Angeles, which includes surrounding towns and counties, embraces about 16 million people. In the center of this sprawl is the city of Los Angeles, with City Hall rising from its downtown heart.

Much of this region's spectacular growth has taken place in the last sixty years. In 1940, Los Angeles proper was America's fifth largest city. Today, it ranks second in terms of population. Shopping malls and high-rise buildings stand where orange groves used to bask in the sun. Highways run everywhere to link far-flung communities.

Los Angeles sits on the Pacific Ocean in southern California. People often call it by its initials, LA (pronounced *el ay*). It is an industrial giant, with more than 25,000 factories. LA produces movies, clothing, airplanes, spacecraft, high-tech computers, and other products as modern as tomorrow. Its industries have created millionaires. However, masses of people live in poverty. Gang warfare, homelessness, and drugs are pressing problems in Los Angeles. Too many automobiles have given Los Angeles the most polluted air of any big city in the United States. Add shaky ground to this list of woes. Deadly earthquakes rocked Los Angeles in 1971 and again in 1994.

Hollywood jacket patch of a cameraman filming a movie

The Los Angeles City Hall

Yes, LA has a host of problems. But it is also a city of promise. Why else would people from around the world flock there to live? Residents, called Angelenos, freely discuss their city's merits as well as its demerits. Just about everyone agrees that LA is never a boring place. It is home to the movie and television industries, perhaps the most exciting businesses in the country. Few other cities have such ethnic diversity. More than 80 different languages are spoken on the streets. Restaurants serve meals ranging from Mexican tacos to Japanese sushi.

The city's gentle climate promotes an outdoor lifestyle. Miles of public beaches front the Pacific Ocean and serve as a gigantic municipal swimming pool.

Everyone who has ever been there harbors an opinion of Los Angeles. By any measure, it is an interesting city, a fun place to study. A good spot to begin a study of LA is at its center.

A beach at Malibu

GREAT CITY

"Los Angeles . . . where mankind devours every habitable place and then sprawls farther and farther out into the desert . . ."
—From *The Book of America*, written in 1983.

GRASPING THE GIANT

Near City Hall is Olvera Street, which is given over to a pleasant Mexican market. Vendors operating from tiny stands sell handmade leather belts, juicy tacos, and the delightful *piñatas* that children break to retrieve candy and other treats hidden inside. Olvera Street is the city's oldest street. Immigrants from Mexico first settled there more than two hundred years ago. Historically at least, Olvera Street is the city's beginning. Where the gigantic city ends is quite another question.

Olvera Street lies in the heart of downtown LA. From this spot, the city grew into today's huge metropolitan region. To grasp an idea of this giant, think of a stone dropped in a pond of water. The splash creates circles expanding outward. Consider the inner circle, the smallest of them, as the city of Los Angeles. The next circle, somewhat larger, is Los Angeles County. The third and biggest of the circles is the vast area usually called Greater Los Angeles. All three circles make up the Los Angeles metropolitan region, the second largest population center in the United States.

Hispanic boys in traditional hats and clothing at a Cinco de Mayo festival

Hispanic folk dancers performing in colorful traditional dresses

The city of Los Angeles, the area defined by its city limits, is huge as cities go. Los Angeles proper spreads over 466 square miles (1,207 square kilometers). This makes it, in area, twice the size of Chicago. The city consists of downtown and seven recognized neighborhoods—South-Central, Central, the San Fernando Valley, West Los Angeles, South Bay, Port of Los Angeles, and East Los Angeles. Unlike people in other cities, Angelenos do not have to "go downtown" to work or to shop. Still, downtown is the hub of the city, and it has undergone extensive rebuilding in recent years.

Visitors enjoying all that Olvera Street has to offer

Los Angeles County is an enormous region. In area, the county is almost the size of the entire state of Connecticut. More than 80 independent towns, lying outside the LA city limits, make up Los Angeles County. Some 9 million people live within Los Angeles County. It is the most populous county in the United States. The city of Long Beach alone holds almost 450,000 people. Long Beach is the second largest city in the Los Angeles region, and it ranks fifth in the state of California.

Greater Los Angeles is the last circle in this ever-expanding giant. This region takes in five counties—Los Angeles, Orange, Riverside, San Bernardino, and Ventura. More than

A wall mural on Balboa Island

650 miles (1,046 km) of super-highways (called freeways) lace the area. But don't expect to see distinct communities when driving along the freeways.

Greater Los Angeles is a blend of buildings, roadways, shopping malls, and parking lots. This situation has lent itself to the famous quote that Los Angeles is really "one hundred suburbs in search of a city."

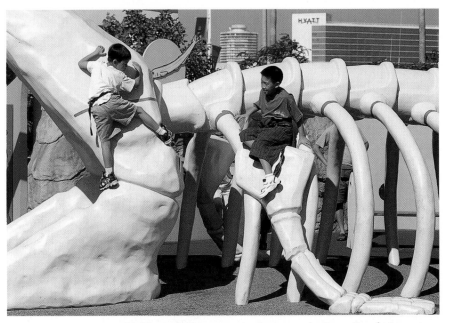

Children climbing on a sculpture at the Long Beach Aquarium

Hooray for Hollywood

Of course, the most glamorous Los Angeles neighborhood is the movie capital of Hollywood. Companies began making movies there in 1911. By the 1930s and 1940s, Hollywood was hailed as the screen wonderland of the world. Today, TV shows and TV commercials are filmed in Hollywood. Because of its glitz and glitter, Hollywood is often called "Tinseltown." The great white sign HOLLYWOOD was erected on Mount Lee in 1923 and is now Tinseltown's renowned symbol.

THE ANGELENOS

Hungry? Go to LA's Chinatown to enjoy great meals. However, you will find that many of the restaurants have menus written only in Chinese. Ask for a knife and fork and the waiter shrugs his shoulders, a gesture that says, "Here we eat with chopsticks." Chinatown in Los Angeles caters largely to the city's Chinese community. Of course, all customers are welcome in restaurants and shops, but you'd better learn to adhere to Chinese rules.

Costumed children in the Chinese New Year Golden Dragon Parade

Chopsticks and a rice dish

Alhambra is a small community surrounded by the Los Angeles sprawl. Walk the streets there for a lesson in the international makeup of LA's population. Several blocks are crammed with Mexican taco stands. Next, the sidewalks are lined with Chinese and Korean grocery stores. The speech, the signs, even the smells in the air shift as you walk from block to block. A white person entering a supermarket in Alhambra quickly learns what it feels like to be a member of a minority race.

The Los Angeles region has one of the most diverse ethnic populations found any place on earth. Ethnically, Los Angeles County consists of 41 percent Hispanics (mostly Mexicans), 35 percent whites, 12 percent Asians, 10 percent African Americans, and 2 percent Native Americans and others. Demographers (men and women who study population trends) claim that LA is the city of the future. According to demographers, more and more communities in the United States will be like Los Angeles in that they will have no clear majority race. Many Americans believe this is a healthy trend. Without a majority group, there will be no minority group to be cast aside and discriminated against.

A young Hispanic resident of Los Angeles

A ceremonial gate marks the entrance to LA's Chinatown.

Chinese fortune cookies

Equally diverse is the economic status of the Angelenos. Consider Beverly Hills, home of the movie stars. There are sections of Beverly Hills, along Sunset Boulevard or Bedford Drive, where even the smallest house is valued at more than $1 million. Then consider East Los Angeles, a mostly Mexican community where a majority of the people hold factory or laboring jobs. These working-class families do not live in fancy homes, but most have high hopes for the future. The South-Central section is home to almost a half-million African Americans, many of whom are also working-class people. Residents regard South-Central as a community on the rise. South-Central boasts a major shopping mall and the huge theater complex owned by basketball great Magic Johnson.

LA is a study in contrasts, a place where the fabulously rich live within a few miles of the poor and struggling workers. Yet every day, hundreds of people move to LA to take advantage of the opportunities its economy presents. Only about half the present population were born in the Los Angeles region.

Friends

Left: An elegant home in Beverly Hills

Below: The Beverly Hills Hilton hotel

Many of those people who come to the city eventually find the fulfillment of their dreams. Hispanics especially look upon LA as a place of hope. It is estimated that the city's Mexican community sends $6 billion each year to their families in Mexico. Greater Los Angeles has more successful suburban-living African-American people than anywhere else in the United States. African-American women in Los Angeles are established in the professions and many hold high-ranking teaching and government jobs.

GIFTS OF NATURE

Take a morning swim at Laguna Beach in Orange County. Then drive perhaps two hours into the San Bernardino National Forest. There, you can ski downhill slopes in the winter months. The Los Angeles region is one of the few places in the world where a person can swim on a silvery beach and ski on a snowcapped mountain all in the same day.

The greatest natural treasure of Los Angeles is its gentle climate. Sunshine is the norm. Residents expect their days to be bright and sunny. Winter and summer seasons have few cruel extremes. The average temperature in January is 55 degrees Fahrenheit (13° Celsius), and the average in July is 73 degrees Fahrenheit (23° C). LA's pleasant winters are especially admired by Americans who live in the Midwest and the East. Every New Year's Day, the Rose Bowl Parade winds

through the streets of Pasadena in Los Angeles County. People in snow-bound cities such as Detroit or Cleveland watch the parade on television and marvel that those lucky Angelenos can sit outside in T-shirts during January.

There are flaws—human-made and natural—in this pretty picture. First, Los Angeles just does not have enough rainfall.

An average of 15 inches (38 centimeters) of rain a year falls on LA. New York City enjoys almost three times that much rain. Over the decades, a complex system of aqueducts has been constructed to keep the residents supplied with water. Second, Angelenos breathe some of the most polluted air in the nation. Automobiles are

Mormon Rocks, San Bernardino National Forest

the biggest culprits. More than 5 million cars jam the roadways. Angelenos consider the automobile to be an extension of their homes. Institutions such as the attached garage and the drive-in restaurant were born here. Heroic efforts have been made in recent years to clean up auto emissions. But Angelenos remain dependent on cars to get around their huge region, and they often choke on the fumes.

Left: A hazy downtown LA skyline on a smoggy day
Below: Downtown LA on a clear day

Left: Santa Monica Beach

Below: A hiker in the Santa Monica Mountains

Los Angeles County has more than 75 miles (121 km) of shoreline and sports some 30 public beaches. Every Angeleno has a favorite beach, and every beach has character of its own. Venice Beach is the original "muscle beach," where men proudly display bulging biceps. Will Rogers State Beach is a favorite family spot. Mountainous waves at Malibu Beach lure surfers. Many Angelenos hail Zuma Beach as the region's prettiest stretch of sand and sea.

From the sunny beaches, a bather can look to the east and see forested or snowcapped mountains. Just a few miles inland stands Mount San Antonio (nicknamed Old Baldy), which rises more than 10,000 feet (3,048

Binoculars like these are used by children who hike with their parents in the Santa Monica Mountains.

The Santa Monica Mountains National Recreation Area

Spreading over 150,000 acres (60,704 hectares), the Santa Monica Mountains are hailed as the world's largest urban park. More than 600 miles (966 km) of mountain trails cut through this wilderness area. Some 450 animal species—including coyotes, deer, and even mountain lions—make their homes here. Visitors to the park enjoy horseback riding and bird-watching.

meters) above sea level and is the tallest mountain in Los Angeles County. Hiking, skiing, and mountain biking are popular activities in the LA highlands. This great diversity of landscapes is one of the reasons moviemakers moved here years ago. The movie companies were able to film a desert location, a snowy mountain location, or a sunny beach location all within a few hours' drive from their studios.

"As we drew near [the village] we heard violins and guitars . . . we found nearly all the people of the town—collected and crowded together—leaving barely room for the dancers."

— Richard Henry Dana, from his 1842 book *Two Years Before the Mast*. Dana was one of the first Americans to visit Los Angeles, and his report indicates that the Angelenos of old loved to dance and party just as residents do in the modern city.

THE FIRST ANGELENOS

For more than 5,000 years, Native American people lived on this spot where a lazy stream emptied into the Pacific Ocean. That stream was later called the Los Angeles River. The first European to come there was Portuguese sea captain Juan Rodríguez Cabrillo, who was working for Spain. In 1542, Cabrillo sailed along the shore and noted that the river valley was filled with smoke from Indian campfires. Today, critics claim—sarcastically—that even 450 years in the past, LA suffered from polluted air.

Spanish explorers and mission priests came from Mexico in 1769. Mexico at the time was called New Spain and was controlled by the Spanish monarch. One missionary, Juan Crespi, wrote in his journal that the river valley was "a delightful place." Crespi named the spot *El Pueblo de Nuestra Señora la Reina de Los Ángeles del Río Porciúncula*, which means "The Town of Our Lady the Queen of the Angels of the Porciúncula River." Porciúncula was a chapel in Italy. The words *Los Angeles*, meaning "The Angels," remain from the settlement's original name.

A monument to Portuguese sea captain Juan Rodríguez Cabrillo

A Spanish mission in California

The Spanish Missions

Spanish priests built mission churches along the length of California. The churches became centerpieces of small towns called *pueblos*. Several mission churches—including San Gabriel, San Fernando, and San Juan Capistrano— were built in the Los Angeles area. These missions have been tastefully restored and are interesting places to visit. Mission San Juan Capistrano (above), built in 1776 about 60 miles (97 km) southeast of Los Angeles, is known for the swallows that leave every year in October and return to nest in March.

Growth was slow. By 1800, only 70 families living in 30 adobe houses occupied Los Angeles. Even then, the town had a diverse population consisting of whites, blacks, Indians, and people of mixed race. Dramatic upheavals rocked the government to the south. In 1820, the Mexican people concluded a war of independence against Spain and proclaimed Mexico to be an independent nation.

Mexico and the United States went to war in 1846. The war ended in 1848 with the United States claiming all of California and vast tracts of land that once made up Mexico's northern frontier. Then, in 1848, a ranch foreman found a tiny speck of gold in a stream near what is now Sacramento, California. The discovery triggered a human stampede called the Great California Gold Rush. Los Angeles and the American West were transformed forever.

In 1848, before gold was discovered, only about 10,000 people—mostly Mexicans and Native Americans—lived in all of California. By 1850, that number had zoomed to 100,000 and California became the thirty-first state in the American Union. Most of this population boom took place far to the north in the San Francisco and Sacramento area where the goldfields were located. Gradually, the gold-hungry Americans drifted south.

During the 1850s, Los Angeles was a rowdy frontier town. Murders and

Above: The capture of a Mexican battery at Monterey during the Mexican War

Right: Miners panning for gold in a California stream

26

shoot-outs on the streets were common events. Law was often in the hands of a lynch mob. Said one account, "criminals, murderers, bandits, and thieves were hung in accordance with the law or without the law, whichever was most convenient." Sometimes, the violence took an ugly racial tone. In 1871, a white mob stormed through Chinatown, killing 19 Chinese residents. Crime was so rampant that some residents suggested that the city ought to change its name from *Los Angeles* (The Angels) to *Los Diablos* (The Devils).

Civilization came with the railroads. In 1876, tracks linked Los Angeles with San Francisco, and in 1885 a direct line opened to the Midwest. A price war that broke out between railroad companies dropped the cost of a ticket between Los Angeles and Kansas City to a dollar. Railroads brought families. The families built churches and schools. Farmers discovered that oranges grew golden and juicy under the sunny LA skies. Oranges also stayed relatively fresh during the long train trips to eastern cities. By 1890, Los Angeles proper held 50,000 residents. Ten years later, the population had mushroomed to 100,000.

A Cahuenga Valley railroad train in Hollywood

THE BOOM YEARS

Oil was discovered near Los Angeles and soon more than 1,400 derricks were in operation. Thousands of people worked at the Los Angeles harbor as the city became a major ocean port. Factories building airplanes boomed in the 1920s. Movies were the city's magical industry. By the 1930s, the world looked on LA and Hollywood as the place where fantasies came to life. In those days, young and beautiful people journeyed to the city and stood on the famous corner of Hollywood and Vine hoping to be noticed by a movie producer. Few of these promising actors and actresses gained a movie career, but they remembered the thrill of discovering LA.

By 1930, the City of Angels held more than 1 million residents. The city tended to build out rather than up. City Hall, erected in 1928, was LA's only truly tall building. The bungalow became the ideal house for an LA family.

With yards front and back and space on either side, one-family bungalows went up by the thousands in LA and its suburbs. Even in the 1920s, automobiles jammed the roads. But the city was also served by red streetcars that ran down all the major avenues.

Los Angeles and the nation suffered through a terrible business slump in the 1930s. Still, people flocked to the city seeking what few jobs it offered. During World War II (1939–1945), the factories sprang back to life. By the end of the war, Los Angeles was home to more than 1.5 million people.

A huge crowd of people crossing a street in the business district of Los Angeles in 1929

This scene was shot on the set of the 1959 movie Ben-Hur.

The 1950s began a period of prosperity. During the good times, it seemed that every Angeleno wanted a car. To accommodate more vehicles, Los Angeles built its freeway system, the greatest network of roadways ever constructed by any city. Unfortunately, city leaders decided to tear up the venerated streetcar tracks. Public transportation in LA took a backseat to the car.

In the late 1950s and early 1960s, Hollywood studios made a series of beach-party movies. The films showed Angelenos as rich, blond, gorgeous young people who had little else to do but frolic on the beaches. The films were far from the truth, as events would soon prove.

Major earthquakes struck Los Angeles in 1971 and again in 1994. During the 1994 quake, the ground rattled and trembled for a nightmarish 44 seconds. The tremors were deadly reminders that LA sits almost on top of the San Andreas Fault, a line of unstable ground that runs through much of California. The rescue efforts in the 1994 quake were a source of civic pride in racially torn Los Angeles. Perfect strangers, blacks and whites, Hispanics and Asians, worked together to dig out those who were trapped under the rubble of buildings.

Despite the threat of earthquakes, LA began to construct towering office and apartment buildings. Until 1966, the 28-story City Hall was LA's only true high-rise structure. Then, new earthquake-resistant materials were developed and high-rises sprouted like trees. Century City, built in Beverly Hills, is an example of LA's new skyscraper trend. This complex of glass-and-steel office build-

ings went up in what was once the back lot of 20th Century Fox movie studios.

Sadly, the specter of race riots returned to Los Angeles once again. In 1991 a group of white police officers savagely beat a black motorist named Rodney King. Unknown to the police, the beating was captured on video tape by a bystander. It made an ugly scene when presented

on the TV news. About a year later, an all-white jury acquitted three of the officers. Shock and disgust with the jury's verdict triggered a riot that resulted in 53 deaths and 2,400 injuries. During the rioting, a white truck driver was dragged from his cab and beaten almost to the

Above: Rodney King

Left: Rescue personnel looking for survivors of the 1994 Los Angeles earthquake

A night picture of the downtown LA skyline at 8th Street

point of death. This beating, too, was captured on film and presented an ugly scene when aired on the news.

The image of Los Angeles suffered in the wake of riots and earthquakes. No longer did Americans think of LA as a place devoted to beach parties. Still, the city continued to grow and its economy improved. In the late 1990s, LA did the impossible by building a subway in order to reduce residents' dependence on cars. In earthquake-prone LA, the subway was one of the most expensive such projects ever attempted by any city. Yet workers forged ahead and major lines opened in 1999 and 2000. At last, mass public transportation returned to Los Angeles.

In many ways, change is the theme of the LA story. This city has a way of reinventing itself every few decades. Most residents believe that problems will always arise, but they will be solved in time. Meanwhile, Angelenos continue to live, proudly, in an exciting city.

Los Angeles is a place of high culture, music, sports, and entertainment. So much of the city is devoted to pleasure that it is sometimes called "La La Land." Of course, people work and go to school in La La Land as they do everywhere else. But the entertainment scene is special in Los Angeles. This is a city that strives to please.

MUSIC AND THE LIVELY ARTS

According to legend, when Los Angeles was a tiny Mexican village the citizens practiced a delightful custom. The first person up in the morning sang a popular song. As others rose, they joined in. By sunrise, the entire village was up and about and singing to bring in the new day.

Los Angeles is still singing. The city's music scene embraces all tastes—from jazz to rock to classical. On any given night, a concert of some sort is performed. Classical-music lovers go to performances of the Los Angeles Philharmonic Orchestra or the Los Angeles Opera. Rock and pop music is played live in clubs at LA's renovated downtown arts district. West Hollywood is the cool place to go for jazz and blues.

Los Angeles is still the home of the movie industry, and therefore continues to attract young actors and actresses. It is believed that one out of every four professional actors in the nation live in the LA region. However, finding a job in the movies has always been difficult. So the aspiring stars act in theaters. Many prefer to perform before a live audience anyway. Major dramas are presented at the Mark Taper Forum in the Music Center for the Performing Arts in downtown LA. The Dorothy Chandler Pavilion is also part of the Music Center. The Greek Theater in Griffith Park also hosts plays. Small theaters operate downtown and in West Hollywood.

The Pasadena Playhouse in Pasadena is one of the finest theaters in Greater Los Angeles.

The Dorothy Chandler Pavilion at the Music Center for the Performing Arts is host to the annual Academy Awards ceremony.

The people of Los Angeles enjoy a lively world of art. Galleries such as the Ferus Gallery display the works of artists. The 1997 opening of the Getty Center, a billion-dollar collection of paintings and sculptures, was an unforgettable chapter in the LA art scene. More than 1.8 million visitors crowded into the Getty Center during its first year of operation. Hispanic artists, who excel in murals (wall paintings) and other public art, have a wide following.

Hispanic mariachi singers performing on Cinco de Mayo

The Hollywood Bowl

Constructed in 1922, the Hollywood Bowl is an outdoor amphitheater that seats 17,000 people. It is the summertime home of the Los Angeles Philharmonic Orchestra. For generations, Angeleno families have come here to enjoy evening concerts under the stars. The Hollywood Bowl Museum, which is on the grounds, traces the history of this revered building.

SPORTS AND THE GREAT OUTDOORS

The Los Angeles region has two baseball teams (the Dodgers and the Angels) and two pro basketball teams (the Lakers and the Clippers). Over the years, these teams have enjoyed great success. Baseball's Dodgers won their first World Series in 1959, and they fielded a stellar

Above: An LA Dodgers baseball cap
Left: Dodger Stadium

team through most of the 1980s. One of the stars of the '80s Dodgers was Mexican pitcher Fernando Valenzuela. The streets of LA's Hispanic communities went eerily silent when Valenzuela took the mound because nearly everyone was inside watching their TVs. Basketball's Lakers, led by their magnificent guard Earvin "Magic" Johnson, won a string of championships in the 1980s. In the 1999–2000 season, the Lakers rallied behind powerful center Shaquille O'Neal to win the NBA championship.

Pro football has been somewhat of a disappointment in the city in recent years. Generations of fans cheered for the LA Rams of the National Football League (NFL), but the team moved to St. Louis in 1995. The LA Raiders also came and went. By the year 2000, Los Angeles had no NFL team. However, football fans turned their attention to the college game and two regional powerhouses—the University of Southern California (USC) and the University of California at Los Angeles (UCLA). The USC Trojans play at the city's Coliseum while the UCLA Bruins take the field at Pasadena's Rose Bowl. Once a year, the Bruins play the Trojans in what amounts to a civil war for the loyalty of LA fans.

*USC's John Fox during a game
between USC and UCLA*

The most spectacular international sports presentation is the Summer Olympic Games, held once every four years. LA is the only city to have hosted two of these events—in 1932 and again in 1984. The Los Angeles Memorial Coliseum (built in 1923) was the main field for both games. LA Mayor Tom Bradley confessed that as a teenager in 1932, he lacked the money to buy a ticket. So the young Bradley sneaked into the Coliseum by climbing over a wall. Some fifty years later, he opened the games as mayor.

Beach volleyball (below) and in-line skating (right) are popular LA-area sports.

Angelenos are devoted to exercise and individual sports. Los Angeles County has more than 200 miles (322 km) of designated bike trails. Venice Beach is the region's in-line skating capital. Skaters whiz over the Ballona Creek Trail, an 8-mile (13-km) paved route through Venice Beach that is free from vehicular traffic. Inner-city basketball courts are crowded with children. Fishing enthusiasts say the best nearby lakes are Big Bear and Arrowhead in the San Bernardino National Forest. Horseback riding is fun in Griffith Park.

Los Angeles beaches are more than just places to swim. They are also social centers where residents gather, talk, picnic, or people watch. Some beaches are outdoor gymnasiums complete with volleyball nets and playgrounds for small children. The popular Santa Monica Beach boasts an amusement park with a roller coaster. Outdoor weight-lifting—"pumping iron"—is a classic activity at Venice City Beach.

A Venice City Beach body builder

A hand weight like those used in body building

ENJOYING THE GLITZ

As everyone knows, Los Angeles is the land of millionaires and movie stars. Yet you don't have to be rich and famous to enjoy the grandeur there. Window-shopping costs nothing. Stargazing—hoping to catch a glimpse of a screen idol—is also virtually free. Many visitors come to LA to look at riches from afar and to wonder how the privileged set really lives.

Shop where the stars shop on Rodeo (pronounced *roh-DAY-oh*) Drive. This trendy avenue of high-priced stores runs through fashionable Beverly Hills. If you wish (and if your budget allows), you can buy a pair of socks here for a mere $200. Browsing on this exclusive street is interesting even if you buy nothing. And—gasp!—in recent years, a few inexpensive T-shirt and hat stores have appeared on Rodeo Drive.

Perhaps you'll see a star picking through heads of cabbage at LA's famous Farmers Market. But more than likely, the star will send his or her trusted house servant to perform that task. The Farmers Market

Exclusive shops on Rodeo Drive in Beverly Hills

Mann's Chinese Theater

A Beverly Hills arm patch

opened in the city's Fairfax District in 1934 to enable farmers to sell fresh produce to city dwellers. It has now grown to 160 stalls and restaurants. Stars do come here because it is close to CBS Television City headquarters and its restaurants sell exotic international foods.

For decades, tour buses took out-of-towners down Wilshire Boulevard in Beverly Hills while guides pointed out the mansions of the movie idols. Eager tourists looked left and right hoping to catch sight of Bob Hope or some other luminary throwing out his garbage.

This is stargazing, a practice that is very much alive in modern LA. You can identify with the stars of yesterday by visiting Mann's Chinese Theater in the heart of Hollywood. Outside this theater, some 160 movie celebrities have left their handprints and footprints in wet cement. Today, tourists match their feet or hands with those of screen legends such as Humphrey Bogart, Frank Sinatra, and Marilyn Monroe. Cowboy star Gene Autry put the hoofprints of his horse, Champion, here. The old-time comic Jimmy Durante marked the pavement with his signature nose.

Tourists can stargaze by visiting studios or by arranging to see live TV shows. Guests have to wait in long lines in order to see a TV show in the making. But they endure the lines because stargazing remains a strong force in Los Angeles.

LOS ANGELES

Greater Los Angeles covers five counties and spreads over more than 34,000 square miles (88,060 sq km). This makes it roughly the same size as the entire European nation of Austria. Organization is necessary to make even a brief tour of this huge region. Try planning your visit in three steps: step one, Los Angeles proper (within the city limits); step two, LA County; step three, the Greater Los Angeles area.

A LOOK AT THE CITY

Los Angeles has a center, despite what critics say. That center is downtown, a region that was once shabby but is now enjoying a revival. Near the heart of downtown is El Pueblo Historic Park. This park is dedicated to the Spanish pioneers who settled the city in 1781. Chinatown and Little Tokyo are nearby and fun places for

lunch. Stop in at the California Science Center, an exciting museum where kids love the hands-on exhibits. Also downtown is the Natural History Museum of LA County, which features a spectacular Dinosaur Hall. Inside stand the fearsome dinosaur skeletons that children love.

LA's neighborhoods have unique characters that reflect the good and the sometimes cruel aspects of big-city life. Almost 90 percent of the people who live in East LA are of Mexican heritage. All told, Los Angeles holds about 900,000 Mexican people, making it the second-largest Mexican city after Mexico City itself. Residents call East LA the *barrio*, a Spanish word for "neighborhood." East LA extends well beyond the city limits into LA County. Life can be tough in the barrio, but the residents have worked together to build strong community institutions. The Plaza De La Raza in the neighborhood's Lincoln Park is a school that gives children classes in theater, dance, and the arts. Mariachi Plaza is devoted to the lively Mexican bands that play for pay at nearby restaurants. South Central

Shoppers (left and above) on Olvera Street in LA's historic El Pueblo de Nuestro Señora la Reina de Los Angeles district

This mural on a wall at Soto Street and Cesar Chavez Avenue in Boyle Heights is part of the Great Walls Unlimited program.

LA is one of the nation's largest African-American communities. Though torn by crime, the district has many appealing aspects. The California African American Museum specializes in paintings and sculptures by black artists. The Watts Towers represents the work of an Italian immigrant who spent 33 years creating fantastic towers out of discarded soda pop bottles and scrap metal.

Walls of Art

In 1988, the city sponsored a program called Great Walls Unlimited: Neighborhood Art. The program gathered the city's best artists and set them to work brightening neighborhoods by painting murals on outdoor walls. Hispanic artists in East LA led the show, but African-American artists in the South Central section and Korean painters in Koreatown also created sparkling murals. One mural, completed in 1976, is called the Great Wall of Los Angeles. It is 2,500 feet (762 m) long and tells the history of California from prehistoric times to the present.

Central Los Angeles includes the glitter of Hollywood. Movie lovers take the Hollywood Walk of Fame, called the "world's most famous sidewalk." Along this sidewalk are granite slabs embedded with golden stars and the names of famous movie personalities—Marlon Brando, Louis Armstrong, Barbra Streisand—and some 2,500 others. Sunset Boulevard runs through Central LA. The section called Sunset Strip is lined with trendy restaurants and shops.

More than a million people live in LA's San Fernando Valley. Known often as the "Valley," it is made up largely of single-family homes. For the most part, the Valley is a prosperous community and many homes have backyard pools. Car culture is prevalent here. Some claim the Valley gave birth to institutions such as the drive-in bank and drive-in restaurant. A highlight of the San Fernando Valley is the Mission San Fernando Rey de España. One of California's original missions, it was founded by Spanish priests in 1797. The mission has been lovingly restored. Inside are marvelous examples of Native American art and crafts.

Don't miss the other museums offered in the city. The California Museum of Science and Industry honors the state's agriculture and manufacturing enterprises. Modern art is featured at the Museum of Contemporary Art. Two LA museums are dedicated to moviemaking: the Hollywood Wax Museum and the Hollywood Studio Museum. In 1988, Western movie star Gene Autry founded the Gene Autry Western Heritage Museum, which profiles the Old West. An exciting place to visit is La Brea Tar Pits. Some 40,000 years ago, Ice Age animals got trapped on these gooey grounds. More than 1 million animal bones have been excavated at the Tar Pits. You can see re-creations of the long-ago beasts, including the fierce saber-toothed tiger.

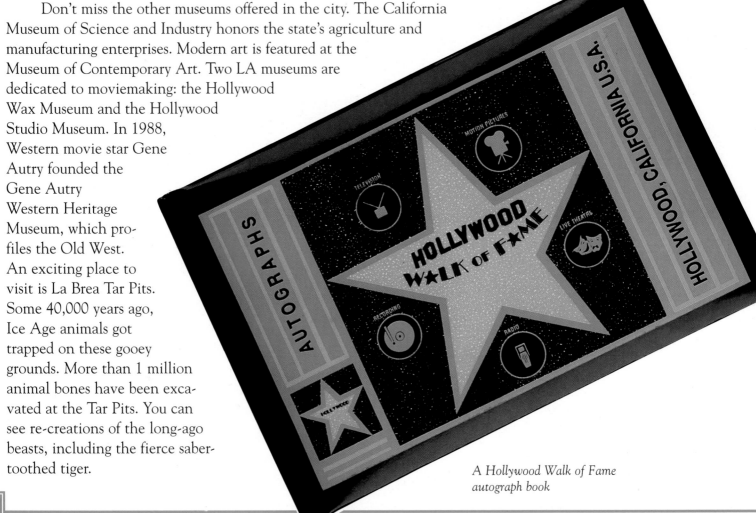

A Hollywood Walk of Fame autograph book

An exhibit at La Brea Tar Pits

Griffith Park

Spreading over 4,000 acres (1,619 ha), Griffith Park is the nation's largest city park. It is twice the size of New York City's Central Park. The land was donated to the city years ago by Griffith J. Griffith, a Scottish immigrant who made millions in gold dealing. There are more than 210 parks in the city, but Griffith remains the favorite of Angelenos. Within the park are the Greek Theater, the Griffith Observatory and Planetarium, and the Los Angeles Zoo.

LOS ANGELES COUNTY AT A GLANCE

Signs tell drivers where the city ends and LA County begins. Without the signs, it would be difficult to tell the difference in this ocean of malls and highways. In the early 1900s, the towns of LA County were distinct. Many towns were surrounded by farms or orange groves. Today, suburban expansion has gobbled up the farms. Still, the towns retain some of their old-time individual character.

Pasadena is a prosperous community that rests at the base of the San Gabriel Mountains. Old Town Pasadena offers a glimpse of the city as it existed before it became surrounded by the LA sprawl. The Norton Simon Museum in Pasadena has an outstanding collection of European art. Not to be missed are Pasadena's Pacific Asia Museum and the Huntington Library, Art Collections, and Botanical Gardens.

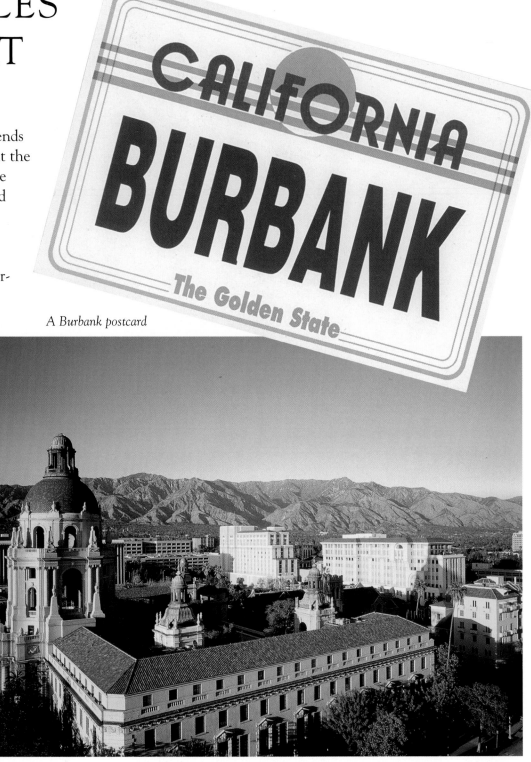

A Burbank postcard

A view of the Pasadena City Hall and the San Gabriel Mountains

Holding some 180,000 people, Glendale is LA County's third largest city. Many of Glendale's houses were built in the 1920s, when the town thrived as a suburban LA community. Today, Glendale is famed for its Forest Lawn Cemetery, where movie greats of the past are buried. Resting at Forest Lawn are notables such as Walt Disney, Humphrey Bogart, Errol Flynn, Larry Fine (one of the Three Stooges), and L. Frank Baum (author of *The Wizard of Oz*).

For years, the LA County community of Burbank was the brunt of jokes. A popular TV comedy show of the 1960s called *Laugh In* used to say, with a snicker, "We broadcast from beautiful downtown Burbank." Today, however, Burbank is home to some of the world's most important movie and TV studios. Columbia Pictures, Warner Brothers, and Disney all have studios in Burbank. Aspiring young performers arrive in Burbank hoping to be discovered. Visitors tour Burbank's studios and are thrilled to see the places where miracles are made.

The city of Long Beach is aptly named because it has about 10 miles (16 km) of seashore. Tourists arrive here to climb on board the *Queen Mary*, once the most elegant ocean liner on the seas. The *Queen Mary* is now retired and docked permanently at Long Beach where it reminds visitors of what the words "luxury liner" ought to mean. The Aquarium of the Pacific opened in Long Beach in 1998. More than 12,000 sea animals are displayed, ranging from fearsome-looking sharks to delicate sea horses.

The luxury liner Queen Mary *is now docked at Long Beach.*

Not all of LA County is lost in a swirl of suburban development. The San Gabriel Mountains contain the Angeles National Forest, a playground for some 30 million visitors a year. Most of the people who hike the trails or ski the slopes at San Gabriel are locals. This wonderful wilderness area is curiously undiscovered by out-of-town visitors. However, tourists ought to take a wilderness adventure in the lovely Angeles National Forest, which lies just a few minutes drive from the teeming big city.

Above: Delicate sea horses like this one can be seen at the Aquarium of the Pacific in Long Beach.

GREATER LOS ANGELES

If greater Los Angeles were a state, it would be roughly as large as South Carolina, which ranks fortieth in size of the fifty states. This huge area contains many towns which in recent years have become looked upon as suburbs of the City of Angels. Yet residents know that their communities are places with personalities distinct from the big city.

Friends in LA

Do you like to surf
or at least watch surf-
ing? Huntington Beach
in Orange County is a
magnet for wave riders
from around the world.
The seashore of Orange
County is often called the
Orange Coast. Seal Beach,
Sunset Beach, Newport
Beach, and Laguna Beach
are other popular
Orange Coast spots.
The Bolsa Chica
Ecological Reserve
along the Orange
Coast is a salt marsh
that supports more
than 200 bird species.

*A starfish found
on an LA beach*

*The beautiful Los Angeles area beaches are
magnets for residents and tourists alike.*

*A young family enjoying
an LA area beach*

Anaheim is the oldest and largest city in Orange County. It was founded in 1857 by German settlers who combined the name "Ana" from the Santa Ana River and "heim" from the German word for home. The city is now a convention and tourist center that boasts more than 40,000 hotel rooms.

Anaheim's biggest attraction is everyone's favorite place to visit—Disneyland.

In 1955, Walt Disney carved his fantasy world out of an orange grove about 28 miles (45 km) southeast of Los Angeles. Today, Disneyland spreads over 76 magical acres (32 ha) and delights guests with its famous theme sections—Main Street USA, Frontierland, Tomorrowland, Adventureland, Fantasyland, and others. Over the years, its rides have gotten scarier. The spinning teacups of a ride called the Mad Tea Party will leave you dizzy, and a plunge down the Matterhorn Bobsleds roller coaster might take your breath away.

Nearby is another amusement park complete with towering roller coasters. Knott's Berry Farm began as a berry farm owned by the Knott family. In 1932, Mr. Knott built a haunted house to entertain local farmhands and their families. Today, Knott's Berry Farm is almost as popular as Disneyland.

Greater Los Angeles spreads beyond Orange County into Riverside, San Bernardino, and Ventura Counties. The region includes more than 170 cities and towns and wilderness areas such as the Cleveland National Forest and the San Bernardino National Forest. The City of Angels and its surrounding communities continue to delight residents and visitors. Most Angelenos believe that, despite its problems, LA is a great place to live.

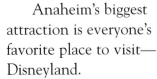

A young East Indian LA resident

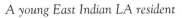

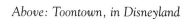

Above: Toontown, in Disneyland

Left: Amusement rides and games at Knott's Berry Farm

FAMOUS LANDMARKS

Far left: The Greek Theater at Griffith Park

Left: The Griffith Observatory

Right: The LA City Hall

City Hall
Until 1966, this graceful building with its pyramid-shaped tower was the tallest structure in Los Angeles. Like many other LA monuments, City Hall has been used as a prop for movies. The building was "blown up" by an alien spacecraft in the 1953 thriller *War of the Worlds*.

Los Angeles Central Library
One of the most recognizable buildings on the city's skyline, the Public Library was constructed in 1930. The library holds 2.5 million books. Murals in the History Room tell the story of California's past. Just outside is the Bunker Steps, a monumental staircase with a stream of water flowing into a pool at its base.

The Bradbury Building
Some Angelenos call the design of this downtown building "quirky." It is a mixture of architectural styles drawn up by an amateur architect in 1893. The architect claimed he was inspired by ideas given to him by his dead brother whom he spoke with via a Ouija board. The Bradbury Building was a prominent setting in both the 1941 mystery film *The Maltese Falcon* and the 1982 science-fiction film *Blade Runner*.

Union Station
Built in 1939, this grand depot harkens back to the days of luxury train travel. The waiting room is capped by a wood-beamed ceiling that towers 52 feet (16 m) high. A food court sells ethnic treats ranging from tacos to bagels. The building was the setting for a 1950 detective thriller appropriately called *Union Station*.

Avila Adobe
Built in 1818, this simple one-story house is LA's oldest standing structure. It was owned by Don Francisco Avila, who was once mayor of the Spanish pueblo called Los Angeles. The house is open to the public and admission is free.

Japanese American National Museum
Situated in the heart of the neighborhood known as Little Tokyo, this museum celebrates 130 years of Japanese immigration to the United States. Volunteers show guests the delicate art of paper folding called origami. Grim photos document the terrible times of World War II when Japanese Americans were imprisoned for fear they were spies for Japan.

Left: Union Station
Below: The famous Hollywood sign

Exposition Park
This was once a fairgrounds where farmers displayed prized cows. Now, it is a public park with many attractions including the Aerospace Museum and the popular Rose Garden.

Universal Studios
Touring a film studio is a highlight of any visit to LA, and Universal Studios is the city's largest. You'll see props used in pictures such as *Jurassic Park* and *Back to the Future*. Amazing special-effects trickery makes visitors to Universal Studios think they are being "attacked" by a giant shark.

The Hollywood Sign
What is perhaps the world's most famous sign stands on the slope of Mt. Lee and can be seen from most of Hollywood's streets. It was first erected in 1923. The sign was marred by tragedy in 1932 when a young actress, depressed because she failed to get a part in a movie, climbed to the top of the letter *H* and jumped to her death.

The Los Angeles Zoo
Spreading over 75 acres (30 ha) in Griffith Park, this delightful zoo is home to some 2,000 animals. The animals are grouped by their geographical regions—North and South America, Africa, Eurasia, and Australia. Included in the collection are 78 endangered species.

The Griffith Observatory and Planetarium
One of the great sky shows offered anywhere can be seen in this famous planetarium. Some narrated shows take an audience on a search for extraterrestrial life, and others—appropriate for Los Angeles—examine the causes of earthquakes. The Planetarium was built in 1935. Fans of film idol James Dean will recognize it as the site where Dean had a fight with the high-school bully in the 1955 movie *Rebel Without a Cause*.

Olvera Street
History comes alive when you walk down Olvera Street in the heart of downtown. The street has 27 historic buildings, some of which date back to the days when Los Angeles was a Mexican pueblo. Now, Mexican handicrafts and tasty foods are served from streetside stalls.

FAST FACTS

POPULATION   1990

City   3,485,398
Greater Los Angeles   16,000,000

AREA

City   466 square miles
                                  (1,207 sq km)
Greater Los Angeles   34,000 square miles
                                  (88,060 sq km)

LOCATION   Los Angeles lies in southern California along the Pacific Ocean.

LAND PROFILE   Greater Los Angeles is a remarkably diverse land region. Land elevation varies from sea level, along the coast, to more than 10,000 feet (3,048 m) above sea level in inland mountains.

CLIMATE   A gentle climate is one of the major reasons people long to live in LA. The average January temperature is 55 degrees Fahrenheit (13° C), and the average July temperature is 73 degrees Fahrenheit (23° C). A lack of rain is a major problem for Los Angeles, as only about 15 inches (38 cm) of rain falls on the city each year.

INDUSTRIES   With more than 25,000 factories, the Los Angeles area is the nation's most productive industrial center. Aviation is a major enterprise. Greater LA has 2,300 factories devoted to making aircraft, spacecraft, and airplane parts. The city also produces clothing, cars and trucks, computers, electrical machinery, glassware, toys, and many other items. TV and movies are LA's most exciting industries.

CHRONOLOGY

1769
Spanish explorers and priests trek north from Mexico and establish the first California settlements in San Diego and Monterey.

1781
El Pueblo de Nuestra Señora la Reina de Los Angeles is founded.

1820
Mexico concludes a war of independence against Spain, and Los Angeles becomes a town within Mexico.

1846
The United States declares war against Mexico.

1848
The U.S.-Mexican War concludes with the United States claiming California and other lands that today comprise the southwestern states.

1849
Thousands of North Americans, Latin Americans, and Chinese rush to northern California in hopes of growing rich in the newly discovered goldfields.

1850
Los Angeles is established as a city.

1876
Railroad tracks are completed linking Los Angeles with San Francisco.

1885
A railroad line is opened connecting Los Angeles directly with the midwestern United States.

1900
LA's population reaches 100,000.

1920s
Moviemaking becomes a glamour industry in the Hollywood neighborhood.

1940s
During World War II (1939–1945), Los Angeles factories produce thousands of airplanes and many other war goods.

1960
LA's population nears 2.5 million.

*Mickey Mouse in
Disneyland*

1965
A riot in the Watts neighborhood pits black people against the police; 34 people are killed and many are injured.

1971
An earthquake rattles Los Angeles, causing 65 deaths and great property damage.

1973
Thomas Bradley, the city's first African-American mayor, is elected; he is reelected to four more terms.

1992
A riot explodes after a jury acquits three police officers who severely beat a black motorist; 53 people are killed during the disorder.

1994
Another major earthquake strikes Los Angeles.

1999
The Red Line on LA's new subway system, called Metro Rail, is opened; the subway is especially costly because it is built to withstand earthquakes.

2000
The LA Lakers win the NBA championship

LOS ANGELES

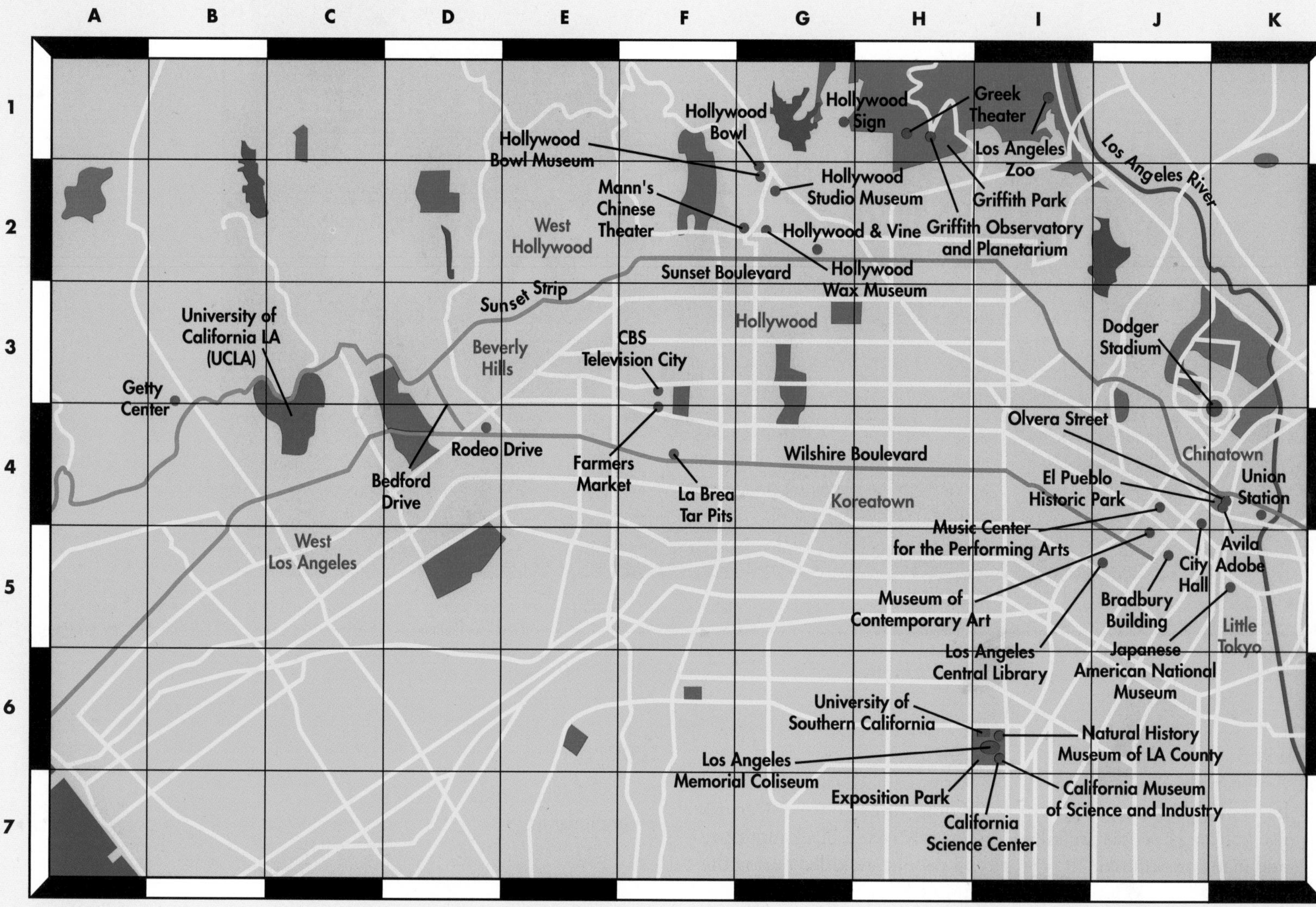
A
B
C
D
E
F
G
H
I
J
K
1
2
3
4
5
6
7
Hollywood Bowl
Hollywood Sign
Greek Theater
Los Angeles Zoo
Los Angeles River
Hollywood Bowl Museum
Hollywood Studio Museum
Griffith Park
Mann's Chinese Theater
Hollywood & Vine
Griffith Observatory and Planetarium
West Hollywood
Sunset Boulevard
Hollywood Wax Museum
Sunset Strip
University of California LA (UCLA)
Hollywood
Beverly Hills
CBS Television City
Dodger Stadium
Getty Center
Olvera Street
Rodeo Drive
Wilshire Boulevard
Chinatown
Farmers Market
Bedford Drive
La Brea Tar Pits
Koreatown
El Pueblo Historic Park
Union Station
Music Center for the Performing Arts
West Los Angeles
Avila Adobe
City Hall
Museum of Contemporary Art
Bradbury Building
Little Tokyo
Los Angeles Central Library
Japanese American National Museum
University of Southern California
Natural History Museum of LA County
Los Angeles Memorial Coliseum
Exposition Park
California Museum of Science and Industry
California Science Center

Alhambra N1
Anaheim O3
Angeles National Forest M-O 1
Aquarium of the Pacific N3
Avila Adobe K4
Ballona Creek Trail L,M 2
Bedford Drive D 3,4
Beverly Hills D,E 3,4
Bradbury Building J5
Burbank M1
California African American Museum M 2,3
California Museum of Science and Industry I6
California Science Center I6
CBS Television City F3
Central Los Angeles M2
Chinatown J,K 4
City Hall J 4,5
Cleveland National Forest N,O 2
Dodger Stadium K 3,4
Disneyland O3
East Los Angeles N2
El Pueblo Historic Park K4
Exposition Park I6
Farmers Market F4
Forest Lawn Cemetery N1
Gene Autry Western Heritage Museum M1
Getty Center B 3,4
Glendale N1
Greater Los Angeles N,O 3
Greek Theater H1
Griffith Observatory and Planetarium H1
Griffith Park G-H 1,2
Hollywood G3
Hollywood Bowl G2
Hollywood Bowl Museum G2
Hollywood Sign G1
Hollywood Studio Museum G2
Hollywood and Vine G2
Hollywood Wax Museum G2
Huntington Beach O4
Huntington Library, Art Collections, and Botanical Gardens N1
Japanese American National Museum K5
Knott's Berry Farm O3
Koreatown G,H 4

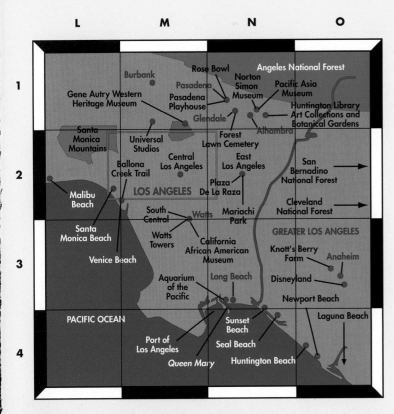

LOS ANGELES & SURROUNDINGS

GLOSSARY

aqueduct: A system of pipes built to transport fresh water

adobe: A house made of sun-dried bricks typically used by Spaniards

bask: To lounge in the sun

culprit: Foe, enemy, or troublemaker

ethnic: Pertaining to a nationality or religious group

excavated: Dug up or unearthed

frolic: To play or have fun

glitz: A slang term meaning exciting or intriguing

luminary: A very important or famous person

pueblo: Spanish name for a town

quirky: Something extremely unusual

sarcastic: A mocking or disapproving attitude

specter: A ghostly or phantomlike image

stellar: Having to do with stars or famous actors or movie personalities

sushi: A Japanese fish delicacy

Picture Identifications

Cover: The skyline of downtown Los Angeles; smiling Hispanic boy
Page 1: Pinocchio interacts with a young visitor at Disneyland, Anaheim
Pages 4–5: The Los Angeles skyline as seen from the lake and fountain in Echo Park
Pages 8–9: Residences along Aliso Beach in South Laguna, Orange County
Pages 22–23: *A Rush for the New Diggings* (California gold rush)
Pages 34–35: Small World, Disneyland
Pages 44–45: Exposition Park rose garden

Photo Credits ©

Liaison Agency — Kathleen Campbell, cover (background), 19 (both pictures); Wesley Hitt, 37 (bottom); Spencer Grant, 51 (left); Eric Sander, 59

Photo Edit — Myrleen Cate, cover (foreground), 40 (right), 54; David Young-Wolff, 4–5, 10, 11 (top), 15 (right), 16; Jonathan Nourok, 37 (top); George Rose, 49 (bottom)

Dave G. Houser — 1, 41 (left), 44–45, 47; Jan Butchofsky-Houser, 11 (bottom), 20 (top), 56 (bottom left); Rankin Harvey, 55 (top)

KK&A, Ltd. — 3, 6 (left), 14 (left), 21 (right), 29 (top), 41 (right), 43 (bottom), 50 (top), 51 (right), 53 (top right), 60, 61

Robert Holmes — 6 (right), 13 (top); Brian McGilloway, 56 (top left)

The Viesti Collection, Inc. — Walter Bibikov, 8–9; Richard Cummins, 12, 14 (right), 33, 34–35, 43 (top)

Visuals Unlimited — Mark E. Gibson, 13 (bottom), 15 (left)

Unicorn Stock Photos — Steve Bourgeois, 17 (top); Bachmann, 40 (left), 53 (bottom right); Eric R. Berndt, 42; Jean Higgins, 49 (top); Chromosohm/Sohm 56 (right); Tommy Dodson, 57 (left)

H. Armstrong Roberts — R. Kord, 17 (bottom)

Corbis — Bob Rowan, Progressive Image, 18; Kelly Harriger, 20–21 (bottom); Nik Wheeler, 24 (right), 55 (bottom); Robert Holmes, 25; Bettmann, 27; UPI/Corbis-Bettmann, 28, 30 (both pictures), 31, 36; Reuters, 32 (top); Bill Ross, 52–53

Stock Montage, Inc. — 22–23

North Wind Pictures — 24 (left), 26 (both pictures)

Globe Photos — 29 (bottom)

Archive Photos — Reuters/Blake Sell, 32 (bottom)

Major League Baseball trademarks and copyrights are used with permisssion of Major League Baseball Properties, Inc. — 38 (top)

Tony Stone Images, Inc. — Joseph Sohm, 38 (bottom); Ken Biggs, 50 (bottom)

Allsport — Tom Hauck, 39

Jim Whitmer Photography — 46 (left), 52 (left)

New England Stock Photo — Jean Higgins, 46 (right)

Courtesy Karol Western Corporation and Hollywood Chamber of Commerce — 48

R. Peevers — 57, (top right)

Network Aspen — Jeffrey Aaronson, 57 (bottom right)

INDEX

Page numbers in boldface type indicate illustrations

TO FIND OUT MORE

BOOKS

Davis, James E. *Los Angeles*. World Cities series. Milwaukee: Raintree Publishers, 1990.

Fodor's Los Angeles. New York: Fodor's Travel Publications, 1999.

Lace, William W. *The Los Angeles Lakers Basketball Team*. Great Sports Teams series. Berkeley Heights, N. J.: Enslow Publishers, Inc., 1998.

MacMillan, Dianne. *Destination Los Angeles*. Port Cities of North America series. Minneapolis: Lerner Publications Company, 1997.

_____. *Missions of the Los Angeles Area*. Minneapolis: Lerner Publications Company, 1997.

McGrew, Patrick. *Landmarks of Los Angeles*. New York: Harry N. Abrams, Inc., 1994.

Pietrusza, David. *The Los Angeles Dodgers Baseball Team*. Great Sports Teams series. Berkeley Heights, N. J.: Enslow Publishers, Inc., 1999.

Rambeck, Richard. *Los Angeles Clippers*. NBA Today series. Mankato, Minn.: Creative Education, 1998.

St. Peter, Joan. *Los Angeles Kings*. NHL Today series. Mankato, Minn.: Creative Education, 1996.

Salak, John. *The Los Angeles Riots*. America's Cities in Crisis series. Brookfield, Conn.: Millbrook Press, 1993.

Vogel, Carol G. *Shock Waves Through Los Angeles: The Northridge Earthquake*. Boston: Little, Brown and Company, 1996.

ONLINE SITES

California Science Center
http://www.casciencectr.org/
A tour of the museum with information on permanent and special exhibits, visitor information, education programs, and more.

Los Angeles Clippers
http://www.nba.com/clippers/
This official website of the LA Clippers includes draft picks, schedule, player stats, and more.

Los Angeles County
http://www.co.la.ca.us/
This site, which includes a brief history of the county, is an overview of county government plus an events calendar, a picture of the county flag and seal, county services, and more.

Los Angeles Dodgers
http://www.dodgers.com/
The official website of the LA Dodgers has links to an animated website, a non-animated website, and a movie. Also includes information on the schedule; fantasy camp; this day in Dodger history (updated daily); and quite a bit of Dodger memorabilia advertising.

Los Angeles Lakers
http://www.nba.com/lakers/
The official websiste of the 2000 championship LA Lakers includes current news of the team; the schedule; a history of the team; lots of terrific news of the championship celebrations including the parade; new signings; information on how to join the Future Lakers Club; and more.

Los Angeles Zoo
http://www.lazoo.org/
Everything you want to know about the LA Zoo. Includes closeup pictures of many animals such as snow leopards, condors; chimp babies, and a komodo dragon; educational programs; zoo history; special dates—including the Red Ape Rain Forest enterainment calendar; and much more.

UCLA
http://www.ucla.edu/
The University of Southern California homepage, which includes a welcome by Chancellor Albert Carnesale, gives an overview of the school, the campus, history and traditions, a historical tour, answers to frequently asked questions, admissions information, snd much more.

ABOUT THE AUTHOR

R. Conrad Stein was born and grew up in Chicago. At age eighteen he enlisted in the Marine Corps and served three years. He later attended the University of Illinois and graduated with a degree in history. Mr. Stein is a full-time writer, and has published more than 100 books for young readers. He lives in Chicago with his wife, Deborah Kent, also an author of books for young readers, and their daughter Janna.

Traveling is Mr. Stein's passion. The author loves to walk about cities and back roads that he has never seen before. He first visited Los Angeles when he was a young man in the Marines. Mr. Stein has been back many times, and always tries to see a new area of the Greater Los Angeles region. He thoroughly enjoys the City of the Angels.